The Night, They Say, Was Made for Love

plus

My Sexual Scrapbook

Author of

Don't Worry, He Won't Get Far on Foot:
The Autobiography of a Dangerous Man

Do Not Disturb Any Further

Digesting the Child Within

Do What He Says, He's Crazy

I Think I Was an Alcoholic

The Night,
They Say,
Was Made for Love

plus

My Sexual Scrapbook

JOHN CALLAHAN

Quill
William Morrow
New York

For information about Callahan T-shirts, mugs, and other products, please contact:

Levin Represents
Deborah Levin
P.O. Box 5575
Santa Monica, CA 90409

It is the policy of William Morrow and Company, Inc., and its imprints and affiliates, recognizing the importance of preserving what has been written, to print the books we publish on acid-free paper, and we exert our best efforts to that end.

Library of Congress Cataloging-in-Publication Data

Callahan, John.
     The night, they say, was made for love : plus, my sexual scrapbook
by John Callahan.
          p.   cm.
     ISBN 0-688-12648-0
     1. American wit and humor, Pictorial.   I. Title.
NC1429.C23A4   1993
741.5′973—dc20   93-5151
                                                            CIP

Printed in the United States of America

First Edition

1 2 3 4 5 6 7 8 9 10

For Deborah Levin

Acknowledgments

I'd like to thank the following people for their unending help and support: Richard Callahan, Deborah Levin, Larry Wobbrock, Bill McGrath, Jerry Fine, Richard Pine, Larry Kegan, and especially my editor, Liza Dawson.

CALLAHAN

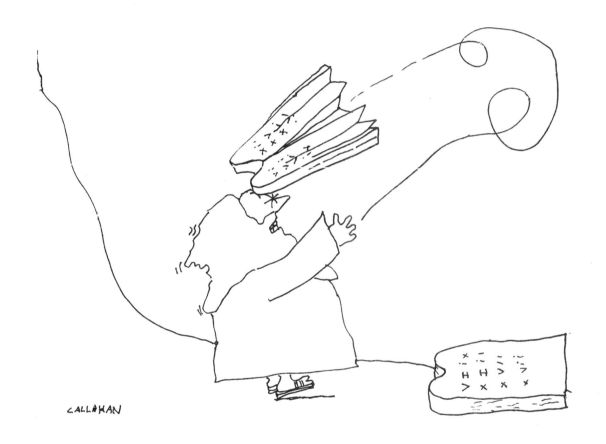

CALLAHAN

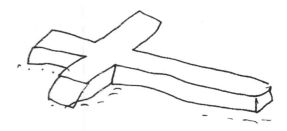

CALLAHAN

"Run for your life! It's the Sally Struthers car alarm!!!"

THE FLATULENT NUN

1. 2.  3.

CALLAHAN

"Janice! Your calf implants look great!!"

MY DINNER WITH HOMBRE

CALLAHAN

"I'm getting a personal trainer!"

"Now remember—spank the bottom, cut the cord,
and check the child for weapons."

CALLAHAN

CALLAHAN

"Space travelers? Hell! We're just looking for a place to have a cigarette."

CALLAHAN

The statue reads: WILLIAM MILLS CONTROL FREAK

"Look, Billy! A bisexual built for two!!"

38

CALLAHAN

When Chuck returned home, his door was a jar.

THE DOLLY LLAMA

CALLAHAN

CALLAHAN

"Yuppies, Kimosabe. Thousands of them!"

"The warden says you'll be eligible for conjugal visits soon!"

"I'm sorry I yelled at you.
There are just certain things you can't put in a juicer."

"Oh, great! That chili's coming back on me!"

CALLAHAN

CALLAHAN

CALLAHAN

"You used to rub up against something when you saw me coming."

"When I touch him he rolls into a ball."

"Who knows George Washington's birthday? Let's see a show of guns."

SPINAL CORD INJURY CENTER

Standing ROOM ONLY

CALLAHAN

"It's a '57 Chevy with chrome wheels, tinted windows,
Hurst 4-shift, and a 283 with dual quads."

"What do you mean, how long am I going to be at this number?!!"

"Okay, everybody, break it up! Haven't you ever seen a starlet
without an exercise video on the market?"

71

"Another outburst like that and I'll have this courtroom cleared!!"

"I'm out of birth control pills—try wearing these."

"Do you feel comfortable talking about the straw?"

**Jesus, Mary, and Joseph and the 3 Wisemans
(Murray, Ruth, and Sid).**

"Why don't you go ahead, honey—I had that placenta this morning."

AFTER CATCHING THE WORM, THE EARLY BIRD BOUGHT A TOWN HOUSE ON THE UPPER WEST SIDE, MARRIED A FEMALE HALF HIS AGE, AND SETTLED INTO BENIGN OBSCURITY. HE TOOK TO DRINK AFTER A SERIES OF PERSONAL SETBACKS, FELL IN WITH A THRILL-SEEKING CROWD, AND WAS SUBSEQUENTLY ARRESTED FOR CERTAIN PERVERSIONS. DESPONDENT, AND WITH HIS MARRIAGE IN SHAMBLES, HE FLEW HEADLONG INTO A PATIO WINDOW, BREAKING HIS NECK.

CALLAHAN

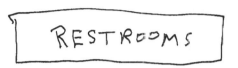

CALLAHAN

CALLAHAN

" Thirty fales moves and you're dead "

Chuck Wilson with the largest refrigerator taken from L. A. River

My
Sexual
Scrapbook

By John Callahan

My initiation to the world of sex came when I first saw my parents' genitals.

For the next few years I wasn't really interested in anything sexual.

As I grew older, my curiosity increased by leaps and bounds. I found answers where I could.

Then came puberty.

Suddenly I found myself experiencing all kinds of intense desires and emotions. The thought of my parents having sex disgusted me.

It was too good to be true.

One day, as I was drying off my penis over and over again, I inadvertently brought myself to orgasm.

I tried it again and again, in several locations.

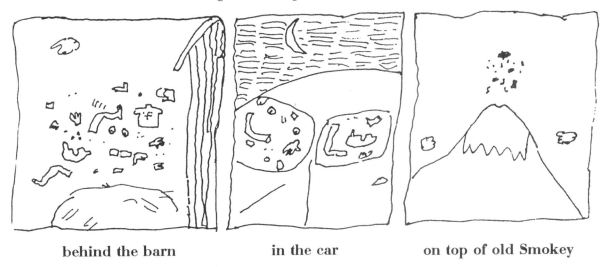

behind the barn   in the car   on top of old Smokey

**I found myself in the grip of a terrible compulsion
which created an awful conflict in me.**

Overwhelmed with guilt, I sought release in the confessional.

But I longed to experience sex with an actual girl. Though I knew very little, I fantasized about it constantly.

My high school human sexuality class only intensified my frustration.

It seemed as if everybody and everything was having sex but me.

I felt self-conscious and awkward around girls. They could sense my eagerness.

Finally I met Ruthie and she set me free.

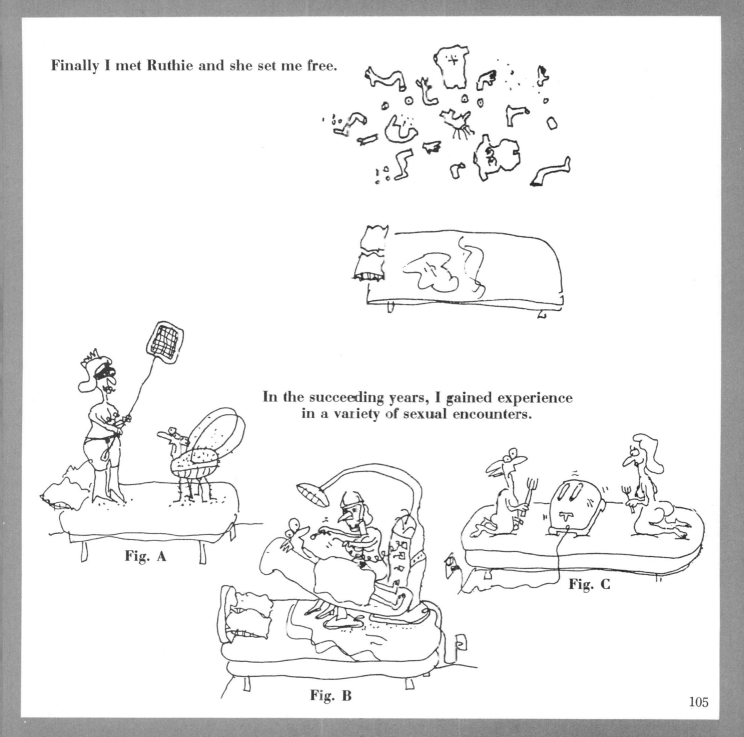

In the succeeding years, I gained experience
in a variety of sexual encounters.

Fig. A

Fig. B

Fig. C

I even began to feel a certain amount
of self-confidence.

When I was paralyzed at twenty-one in a
car wreck, I thought I was finished sexually . . .

But I met a nurse in the rehab center
who was very patient with me.

Soon Jenny and I had a relationship.   Once while making love I had a close call.

Fig. A: Having a good time

Fig. B: Realizing I cannot breathe

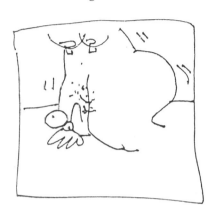

Fig. C: Jenny bears down, misinterpreting my struggle as passion

Fig. E: Release

Fig. D: Panicking at the thought of suffocating

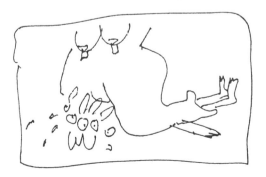

After my paralysis I lost sensation in my lower body, but developed new erogenous zones on top.

Though I try to view women in a healthy way, it is sometimes a real struggle.

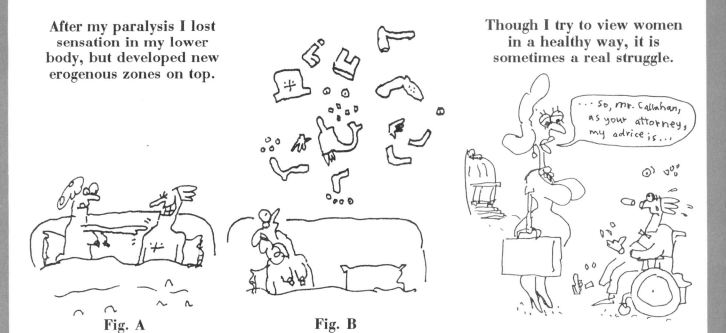

Fig. A

Fig. B

The type of woman I'm attracted to (then and now).

1962   1965   1969   1972   1980   1986   1993

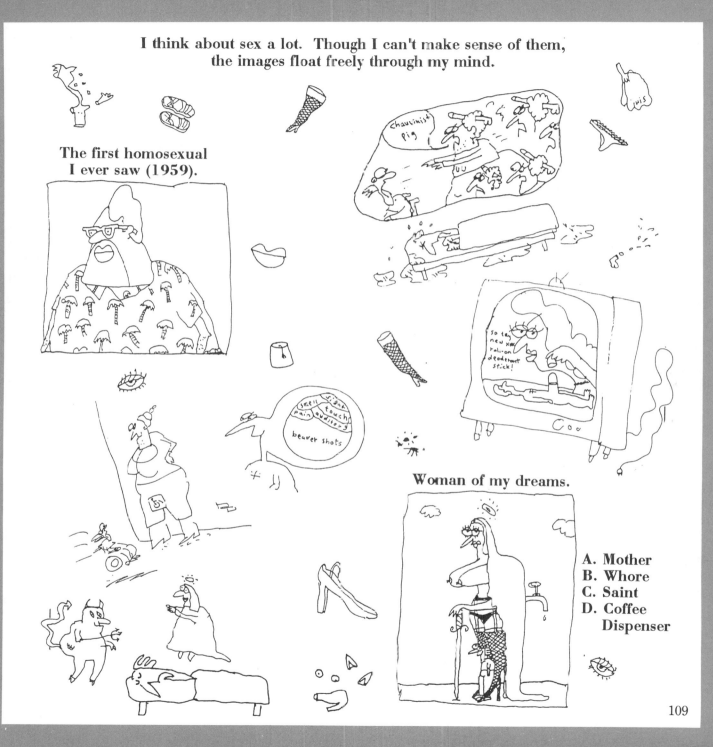

I think about sex a lot. Though I can't make sense of them, the images float freely through my mind.

The first homosexual I ever saw (1959).

Woman of my dreams.

A. Mother
B. Whore
C. Saint
D. Coffee
   Dispenser